"IN THE BEG

A SCRIPTURAL ROSARY
ACCORDING TO
THE PENTATEUCH

by Christine Haapala

Duplettes
by Christine Parson
and Kristiina Ujueta

Suffering Servant Scriptorium
Fairfax, VA
www.sufferingservant.com

Nihil Obstat: Dr. James M. Starke, Ph.D.
Censor Deputatus
Diocese of Arlington
February 14, 2020

The Nihil Obstat is an official declaration that a book or pamphlet is free of doctrinal or moral error. No implication is contained therein that those who granted the Nihil Obstat agree with the contents, opinions, or statements expressed.

The Scripture selections in the Joyful, Sorrowful, and Glorious mysteries were originally published as the 1st Scriptural Rosary in From Genesis to Revelation: Seven Scriptural Rosaries. (ISBN: 0-931886-64-6, 1996; Revised Edition: ISBN: 0-9703996-4-2, 2002)

The fifteen duplettes (art in duality – two pictures in one) originally appeared in the Revised Edition of From Genesis to Revelation: Seven Scriptural Rosaries. Those duplettes were drawn by Christine Parson. Three new duplettes found on pages vii, 18, 22, and 24 were drawn by Kristiina Ujueta.

Cover design and book layout. Alison Ujueta.

ISBN13: 978-0-9840394-8-7
Kindle ISBN13: 978-0-9840394-9-4

Manufactured in United States of America.

DEDICATED TO THE HOLY FAMILY

Thank you to Father Michael Duesterhaus for his unfailing, inspired spiritual direction. Without his guidance, these books would not be possible.

TABLE OF ILLUSTRATIONS

TABLE OF CONTENTS

PREFACE

Dear Brothers and Sisters in Christ,

There are no coincidences, no accidents, and no chance in this life – there is only providence. Providence is when we cooperate with the Lord's grace and use our talents to their best ends. It is not predetermined, nor is something lacking in free will. It is the union of our soul with the will of God.

When reading throughout all of Sacred Scripture, but particularly when reading the Pentateuch – the first five books of the Old Testament – do we see how providence can and has worked. When the Jewish people were faithful to the Lord, when they accepted and followed the Torah, they flourished. And when they failed to work with the Lord, they suffered.

This book couples the path of the Jews to the most common devotion in the Church: the Most Holy Rosary.

This very unique set of meditations should prove to be a great aid to those who are new to the Rosary. It will allow you to help form your thoughts while meditating on the various Mysteries. And to those who have treasured the rosary for many years, you may find in these scriptural insights a fresh approach to your prayers.

No part of our Christian faith is isolated from another: all good devotions draw us to the sacraments and all the sacraments enliven our life in Jesus Christ.

When I was a chaplain with the United States Marines, I would preach about "the broken Rosary." I would tell them upon rising, as part of the morning offering to say the Creed and the first five prayers of the Rosary. Then put it in your pocket. Pray a decade after breakfast. Pray a decade on your way to lunch. Break it up throughout the day. Maybe you may only get to three mysteries on some days. Good. It is better to offer three decades of the rosary – with attention – than attempt to rush through the whole rosary in one setting. And most people do not have the gift of an uninterrupted period of quiet to pray the whole rosary. So break it into parts and squeeze it into your daily life.

And never forget to offer each decade for a different intention. There are always people in need of our prayers, particularly the poor souls in Purgatory.

The Rosary is ultimately "the-Bible-on-beads" – the mysteries are the life, death, and resurrection of our Lord. But they are not just confined to a few passages in the Gospels, for all of scripture is inspired and either is the foundation on which the Gospel stands or is an expression of where the Gospel goes forth after Pentecost. By joining the verses of the Old Testament to the glory of the New Testament the providence of our Lord can clearly be seen.

Pray often. Pray with attention. And pray with fervor.

Fr. Michael R. Duesterhaus
Priest of the Diocese of Arlington, VA

PROPHETIC TRUMPET

The Old Testament prophets trumpeted the prophesies of the coming Messiah. The anticipated birth of the Christ Child in Bethlehem resounded in every hark of their heralding.

"In the Beginning…"

A Scriptural Rosary
according to the Pentateuch

If what you heard from the beginning remains in you, then you will remain in the Son and in the Father. And this is the promise that he made us: eternal life. … His care is to seek the LORD, his Maker, / … To open his lips in prayer, / … and in prayer give thanks to the LORD, / … as he meditates upon his mysteries.
1 Jn 2:24-25, Sir 39:6-7

The Our Father meditations are selected from Sacred Scripture verses that focus on "In the Beginning…" and a reflection on the mystery of the Most Holy Rosary.

The Hail Mary meditations are selected from the Pentateuch [Genesis (Gn), Exodus (Ex), Leviticus (Lv), Numbers (Nm), and Deuteronomy (Dt)]. Additional verses are selected from the Catholic Old Testament books of Wisdom (Wis) and Sirach (Sir).

GABRIEL, THE HOLY SPIRIT'S MESSENGER

The messenger and voice of the Holy Spirit, the archangel Gabriel, appeared to Daniel, as well as, the Blessed Virgin Mary. While Daniel wrote in the Old Testament about the coming Christ, the four Evangelists wrote in the Gospels about the Incarnate Word, the Virgin Mother of the Redeemer, and the Risen Christ.

THE JOYFUL MYSTERIES

The Sign of the Cross
The Apostles' Creed

In the beginning, ... [i]n the beginning was the Word, / and the Word was with God, / and the Word was God. ... We are writing this so that our joy may be complete. *Gn 1:1, Jn 1:1, 1 Jn 1:4*

Our Father...

Abram put his faith in the LORD, who credited it to him as an act of righteousness. *Gn 15:6*

Hail Mary...

You who fear the LORD, hope for good things, / for lasting joy and mercy. *Sir 2:9*

Hail Mary...

"Love the LORD, your God, therefore, and always heed his charge: his statutes, decrees and commandments." *Dt 11:1*

Hail Mary... Glory Be...

WOMAN

Entangled in the serpent's lie, Eve at the foot of a tree brought death to the world as she shared in the first sin with Adam. At the foot of the cross, the New Eve, the Blessed Virgin Mary, crushed the head of the serpent, while the New Adam conquered death.

THE FIRST JOYFUL MYSTERY
THE ANNUNCIATION

When God, in the beginning, created man, / he made him subject to his own free choice. … Mary said, "Behold, I am the handmaid of the Lord. May it be done to me according to your word." … "The first man, Adam, became a living being," the last Adam a life-giving spirit. … Just as we have borne the image of the earthly one, we shall also bear the image of the heavenly one. *Sir 15:14, Lk 1:38, 1 Cor 15:45,49*

Our Father...

God created man in his image; / in the divine image he created him; / male and female he created them. … God looked at everything he had made, and he found it very good. *Gn 1:27,31*

Hail Mary...

[T]he LORD God formed man out of the clay of the ground and blew into his nostrils the breath of life, and so man became a living being. *Gn 2:7*

Hail Mary...

For in the image of God / has man been made. *Gn 9:6*

Hail Mary...

The LORD God said: "It is not good for the man to be alone." … The man called his wife Eve, because she became the mother of all the living. *Gn 2:18, Gn 3:20*

Hail Mary...

For God formed man to be imperishable; / the image of his own nature he made him. / But by the envy of the devil, death entered the world. *Wis 2:23-24*

Hail Mary...

Then the LORD God said to the serpent: / … "I will put enmity between you and the woman, / and between your offspring and hers; / He will strike at your head, / while you strike at his heel." *Gn 3:14-15*

Hail Mary...

"See, I am sending an angel before you, to guard you on the way and bring you to the place I have prepared. Be attentive to him and heed his voice." *Ex 23:20-21*

Hail Mary...

This is the record of the descendants of Adam. When God created man, he made him in the likeness of God. … Adam … begot a son in his likeness … Seth. *Gn 5:1,3*

Hail Mary...

For fear of the LORD is wisdom and culture; / loyal humility is his delight. *Sir 1:24*

Hail Mary...

Humble yourself the more, the greater you are, / and you will find favor with God. *Sir 3:18*

Hail Mary... Glory Be... O My Jesus...

SPIRIT FILLED

All were filled with the Holy Spirit, even those from the womb. Prior to the birth of St. John the Baptist, the Blessed Virgin Mary visited Elizabeth and Zechariah and spent three months helping them. Thirty years later, St. John baptized Jesus in the Jordan River and the Holy Spirit descended and came to rest on Jesus.

THE SECOND JOYFUL MYSTERY
THE VISITATION

Before all ages, in the beginning, he created me, / and through all ages I shall not cease to be. ... O Lord GOD, you have begun to show to your servant your greatness and might. ... Mary said: / "My soul proclaims the greatness of the Lord; / ... He has shown might with his arm, / ... lifted up the lowly." *Sir 24:9, Dt 3:24, Lk 1:46,51-52*

Our Father...

"The God of the Hebrews has sent us word. Let us go a three days' journey in the desert, that we may offer sacrifice to the LORD, our God." *Ex 5:3*

Hail Mary...

"I am God the Almighty. Walk in my presence and be blameless." *Gn 17:1*

Hail Mary...

"[K]eep the commandments of the LORD, your God, by walking in his ways and fearing him. For the LORD, your God, is bringing you into a good country." *Dt 8:6-7*

Hail Mary...

And now, bless the God of all, / who has done wondrous things on earth; / Who fosters men's growth from their mother's womb, / and fashions them according to his will! *Sir 50:22*

Hail Mary...

"May you be blessed in the city, / and blessed in the country! / Blessed be the fruit of your womb." *Dt 28:3-4*

Hail Mary...

But the LORD said to Abraham: "Why did Sarah laugh and say, 'Shall I really bear a child, old as I am?' Is anything too marvelous for the LORD to do?" *Gn 18:13-14*

Hail Mary...

The LORD, your God, has blessed you in all your undertakings; he has been concerned about your journey through this vast desert. *Dt 2:7*

Hail Mary...

"A prophet like me will the LORD, your God, raise up for you from among your own kinsmen; to him you shall listen." *Dt 18:15*

Hail Mary...

"Is this beyond the LORD's reach? You shall see now whether or not what I have promised you takes place." *Nm 11:23*

Hail Mary...

God replied: "Nevertheless, your wife Sarah is to bear you a son, and you shall call him Isaac. I will maintain my covenant with him as an everlasting pact, to be his God and the God of his descendants after him." *Gn 17:19*

Hail Mary... Glory Be... O My Jesus...

SHEPHERD AND KING

Bethlehem, home of King David and his son King Solomon, was the birthplace of the King of Kings. As Mary and Joseph, both of the Davidic lineage, held the Prince of Peace, the three kings, as well as, lowly shepherds adored Jesus. The Good Shepherd's care extends to all of His flock - rich and poor alike.

8

THE THIRD JOYFUL MYSTERY
THE NATIVITY

"The LORD begot me, the first-born of his ways. ... When he established the heavens I was there." ... A star shall advance from Jacob. ... "We saw his star at its rising and have come to do him homage." ... [The magi] saw the child with Mary his mother. ... [They] offered him gifts of gold, frankincense, and myrrh. ... When Herod realized that he had been deceived by the magi, he ... ordered the massacre of all the boys in Bethlehem ... two years old and under. *Prv 8:22,27, Nm 24:17, Mt 2:2,11,16*

Our Father...

Pharaoh then commanded all his subjects, "Throw into the river every boy that is born to the Hebrews." *Ex 1:22*

Hail Mary...

In swaddling clothes and with constant care I was nurtured. ... Pharaoh's daughter ... adopted him as her son and called him Moses; for she said, "I drew him out of the water." *Wis 7:4, Ex 2:10*

Hail Mary...

[T]he glory of the LORD filled the Dwelling. ... "Remove the sandals from your feet, for the place where you stand is holy ground. I am ... the God of Abraham, the God of Isaac, the God of Jacob." *Ex 40:35, Ex 3:5-6*

Hail Mary...

For even his covenant with David, / the son of Jesse of the tribe of Judah, / Was an individual heritage through one son alone; / but the heritage of Aaron is for all his descendants. *Sir 45:25*

Hail Mary...

"I will make of you a great nation, / and I will bless you; / I will make your name great, / so that you will be a blessing." *Gn 12:2*

Hail Mary...

"I will bless those who bless you. ... / All the communities of the earth / shall find blessing in you." *Gn 12:3*

Hail Mary...

You, Judah, shall your brothers praise. ... God acknowledged him as the first-born, / and gave him his inheritance. *Gn 49:8, Sir 44:23*

Hail Mary...

Joy and gladness he will find, / an everlasting name inherit. *Sir 15:6*

Hail Mary...

From every man you shall accept the contribution that his heart prompts him to give me. These are ... gold, ... spices for the anointing oil and for the fragrant incense. *Ex 25:2-3,6*

Hail Mary...

Take up among you a collection for the LORD. Everyone, as his heart prompts him, shall bring ... gold, silver ... violet, purple and scarlet yarn; fine linen ... acacia wood; ... spices for the anointing oil and for the fragrant incense; onyx stones. *Ex 35:5-9*

Hail Mary... Glory Be... O My Jesus...

FIRST BORN, PIERCED WITH A SWORD
In faithful obedience Abraham prepared to sacrifice his first-born son Isaac. Mary and Joseph's obedience to the Mosaic law prefigured the ultimate sacrifice of Christ as "the Lamb of God."

THE FOURTH JOYFUL MYSTERY
THE PRESENTATION OF JESUS IN THE TEMPLE

The beginning of wisdom is fear of the LORD, / which is formed with the faithful in the womb. ... The LORD spoke to Moses and said, "Consecrate to me every first-born." ... When the days were completed for their purification according to the law of Moses, they took [Jesus] up to Jerusalem to present him to the Lord. *Sir 1:12, Ex 13:1-2, Lk 2:22*

Our Father...

"Observe my precepts and be careful to keep my regulations, for then you will dwell securely in the land." *Lv 25:18*

Hail Mary...

"When the days of her purification ... are fulfilled, she shall bring to the priest ... a yearling lamb for a holocaust. ... If, however, she cannot afford a lamb, she may take two turtledoves or two pigeons, the one for a holocaust and the other for a sin offering." *Lv 12:6,8*

Hail Mary...

"On the eighth day she shall take two turtledoves or two pigeons and bring them to the priest at the entrance of the meeting tent." *Lv 15:29*

Hail Mary...

Honor God and respect the priest; / give him his portion as you have been commanded: / First fruits and contributions, / due sacrifices and holy offerings. *Sir 7:31*

Hail Mary...

Throughout the ages, every male among you, when he is eight days old, shall be circumcised. *Gn 17:12*

Hail Mary...

Reflect on the precepts of the LORD, / let his commandments be your constant meditation; / Then he will enlighten your mind, / and the wisdom you desire he will grant. *Sir 6:37*

Hail Mary...

All wisdom is fear of the LORD; / perfect wisdom is the fulfillment of the law. ... "Love the LORD, your God, therefore, and always heed his charge: his statutes, decrees and commandments." *Sir 19:17, Dt 11:1*

Hail Mary...

God also said to Abraham: "On your part, you and your descendants after you must keep my covenant throughout the ages." *Gn 17:9*

Hail Mary...

[T]hen to the place which the LORD, your God, chooses as the dwelling place for his name you shall bring ... every special offering you have vowed to the LORD. *Dt 12:11*

Hail Mary...

"Through those who approach me I will manifest my sacredness; / In the sight of all the people I will reveal my glory." *Lv 10:3*

Hail Mary... Glory Be... O My Jesus...

TEACHER OF WISDOM

Even at an early age, Jesus' wisdom was evident, in particular, during the questioning of the wise men in the temple. At the miraculous feeding of the thousands during the Sermon on the Mount, Jesus also spiritually fed the crowd with words of wisdom. We are also blessed when we hear the word of God and keep it.

THE FIFTH JOYFUL MYSTERY
THE FINDING OF JESUS IN THE TEMPLE

For he gave me sound knowledge of existing things, / ... The beginning and the end and the midpoint of times, / the changes in the sun's course and the variations of the seasons. ... Each year his parents went to Jerusalem for the feast of Passover. ... After three days they found him in the temple, sitting in the midst of the teachers, listening to them and asking them questions, and all who heard him were astounded at his understanding and his answers. *Wis 7:17-18, Lk 2:41,46-47*

Our Father...

For I am your servant, the son of your handmaid. *Wis 9:5*

Hail Mary...

"When your children ask you, 'What does this rite of yours mean?' you shall reply, 'This is the Passover sacrifice ... when he struck down the Egyptians, he spared our houses.'" *Ex 12:26*

Hail Mary...

This day shall be a memorial feast for you, which all your generations shall celebrate with pilgrimage to the LORD, as a perpetual institution. *Ex 12:14*

Hail Mary...

He professes to have knowledge of God / and styles himself a child of the LORD. ... "Assemble and listen, sons of Jacob, / listen to Israel, your father." *Wis 2:13, Gn 49:2*

Hail Mary...

Give new signs and work new wonders; / show forth the splendor of your right hand and arm. *Sir 36:5*

Hail Mary...

He calls blest the destiny of the just / and boasts that God is his Father. ... Peoples will speak of his wisdom, / and in assembly sing his praises. *Wis 2:16, Sir 39:10*

Hail Mary...

Abel, for his part, brought one of the best firstlings of his flock. ... The choicest first fruits of your soil you shall bring to the house of the LORD, your God. *Gn 4:4, Ex 34:26*

Hail Mary...

Moses called all the elders of Israel and said to them, "Go and procure lambs for your families, and slaughter them as Passover victims." *Ex 12:21*

Hail Mary...

Moses, therefore, told the Israelites to celebrate the Passover ... in the desert of Sinai during the evening twilight. *Nm 9:4-5*

Hail Mary...

Take pity on your holy city, / Jerusalem, your dwelling place. / Fill Zion with your majesty, / your temple with your glory. *Sir 36:12-13*

Hail Mary... Glory Be... O My Jesus...
Hail Holy Queen...

SPIRIT FILLED

All were filled with the Holy Spirit, even those from the womb. Prior to the birth of St. John the Baptist, the Blessed Virgin Mary visited Elizabeth and Zechariah and spent three months helping them. Thirty years later, St. John baptized Jesus in the Jordan River and the Holy Spirit descended and came to rest on Jesus.

The Luminous Mysteries

The Sign of the Cross

The Apostles' Creed

In the beginning, when God created the heavens and the earth, the earth was a formless wasteland, and darkness covered the abyss. ... God said, "Let there be light," and there was light. God saw how good the light was. God then separated the light from the darkness. ... In the beginning was the Word, ... / the light shines in the darkness, / and the darkness has not overcome it. *Gn 1:1-4, Jn 1:1,5*

Our Father...

The LORD also told [Moses], "I am coming to you in a dense cloud, so that when the people hear me speaking with you, they may always have faith in you also." *Ex 19:9*

Hail Mary...

Study the generations long past and understand; / has anyone hoped in the LORD and been disappointed? *Sir 2:10*

Hail Mary...

Therefore, you shall love the LORD, your God, with all your heart, and with all your soul, and with all your strength. ... You shall love your neighbor as yourself. I am the LORD. *Dt 6:5, Lv 19:18*

Hail Mary... Glory Be...

RIGHT HAND OF GOD

With the Egyptians in pursuit, Moses and the Israelites crossed the Red Sea and trusted in God's promise to save them and bring them to the Promised Land. The crucified Christ poured forth water and blood to wash us clean. Through His Divine Mercy, He brought salvation and hope in eternal life.

THE FIRST LUMINOUS MYSTERY
THE BAPTISM OF JESUS

"I [am] the Alpha and the Omega, the beginning and the end. To the thirsty I will give a gift from the spring of life-giving water." … God patiently waited in the days of Noah during the building of the ark, … eight in all, were saved through water. This prefigured baptism, which saves you now. … For the LORD, your God, dried up the waters of the Jordan in front of you until you crossed over. … [John] went throughout [the] whole region of the Jordan, proclaiming a baptism of repentance for the forgiveness of sins. *Rv 21:6, 1 Pt 3:20-21, Jos 4:23, Lk 3:3*

Our Father…

In the beginning, … God called the dry land "the earth," and the basin of the water he called "the sea." *Gn 1:1,10*

Hail Mary…

The flood continued upon the earth for forty days. As the waters increased, they lifted the ark, so that it rose above the earth. … Only Noah and those with him in the ark were left. *Gn 7:17,23*

Hail Mary…

Then the LORD said to Moses, … "[L]ift up your staff and, with hand outstretched over the sea, split the sea in two, that the Israelites may pass through it on dry land." *Ex 14:15-16*

Hail Mary…

[T]he LORD swept the sea with a strong east wind throughout the night and so turned it into dry land. *Ex 14:21*

Hail Mary…

[T]he Israelites moved on and encamped in the plains of Moab on the other side of the Jericho stretch of the Jordan. *Nm 22:1*

Hail Mary…

The LORD spoke to Moses. … "Tell the Israelites: When you go across the Jordan into the land of Canaan, … destroy all their stone figures and molten images." *Nm 33:50-52*

Hail Mary…

Hear, O Israel! You are now about to cross the Jordan. … Understand, then, today that it is the LORD, your God, who will cross over before you as a consuming fire. *Dt 9:1,3*

Hail Mary…

The LORD said to Moses: "Take the Levites from among the Israelites and purify them. … Sprinkle them with the water of remission." *Nm 8:5-7*

Hail Mary…

"I myself [Moses] shall die in this country without crossing the Jordan; but you will cross over and take possession of that good land." … "I have let you feast your eyes upon it, but you shall not cross over." *Dt 4:22, Dt 34:4*

Hail Mary…

Joshua, son of Nun, was filled with the spirit of wisdom, since Moses had laid his hands upon him. … Justice and justice alone shall be your aim, that you may have life and may possess the land which the LORD, your God, is giving you. *Dt 34:9, Dt 16:20*

Hail Mary… Glory Be… O My Jesus…

FIRST VINEYARD

God ordained that male and female be as one from the beginning. Because of the sins of mankind, God destroyed all but four couples - Noah and his three sons, and their wives. In celebration of the waters receding, Noah planted the first vineyard. In Cana, Jesus sanctified and celebrated marriage by performing his first miracle by turning water into wine.

THE SECOND LUMINOUS MYSTERY
THE WEDDING AT CANA

Jesus told them, ... "[F]rom the beginning of creation, 'God made them male and female. For this reason a man shall leave his father and mother [and be joined to his wife]'." ... Jesus did this as the beginning of his signs in Cana in Galilee and so revealed his glory, and his disciples began to believe in him. *Mk 10:5-7, Jn 2:11*

Our Father...

[H]e will bless the fruit of your womb and the produce of your soil, your grain and wine and oil. *Dt 7:13*

Hail Mary...

The LORD God then built up into a woman the rib that he had taken from the man. ... [T]he man said: / "This one, at last, is bone of my bones / and flesh of my flesh." *Gn 2:22-23*

Hail Mary...

[Eve] gave birth to a son whom she called Seth. "God has granted me more offspring in place of Abel," she said, "because Cain slew him." *Gn 4:25*

Hail Mary...

The sons of Noah who came out of the ark were Shem, Ham and Japheth. ... [F]rom them the whole earth was peopled. Now, Noah, a man of the soil, was the first to plant a vineyard. *Gn 9:18-20*

Hail Mary...

The LORD took note of Sarah as he had said he would. ... Abraham gave the name Isaac to this son of his whom Sarah bore him. *Gn 21:1,3*

Hail Mary...

Isaac entreated the LORD on behalf of his wife. ... Rebekah became pregnant. ... When the time of her delivery came, there were twins in her womb. ... Esau ... [and] Jacob. *Gn 25:21,24-26*

Hail Mary...

Jacob served seven years for Rachel, yet they seemed to him but a few days because of his love for her. ... [Jacob] was named Israel. God also said to him: / "I am God Almighty; / be fruitful and multiply." ... In a land of grain and wine, / where the heavens drip with dew. / How fortunate you are, O Israel! *Gn 29:20, Gn 35:10-11, Dt 33:28-29*

Hail Mary...

May God Almighty bless you and make you fertile, multiply you that you may become an assembly of peoples. *Gn 28:3*

Hail Mary...

The sons of Jacob were now twelve. The sons of Leah: Reuben, Jacob's first born, Simeon, Levi, Judah, Issachar, and Zebulun; the sons of Rachel: Joseph and Benjamin; the sons of Rachel's maid Bilhah: Dan and Naphtali; the sons of Leah's maid Zilpah: Gad and Asher. *Gn 35:22-26*

Hail Mary...

The LORD, your God, you shall worship; then I will bless your food and drink. ... May God give to you / of the dew of the heavens / And of the fertility of the earth / abundance of grain and wine. *Ex 23:25, Gn 27:28*

Hail Mary... Glory Be... O My Jesus...

TEACHER OF WISDOM

Even at an early age, Jesus' wisdom was evident, in particular, during the questioning of the wise men in the temple. At the miraculous feeding of the thousands during the Sermon on the Mount, Jesus also spiritually fed the crowd with words of wisdom. We are also blessed when we hear the word of God and keep it.

THE THIRD LUMINOUS MYSTERY
THE PROCLAMATION OF THE KINGDOM

Who announced this from the beginning, that we might know; / beforehand, that we might say it is true? … Jesus said to them, "Amen, amen, I say to you, before Abraham came to be, I AM." … Jesus went around to all the towns and villages, teaching in their synagogues, proclaiming the gospel of the kingdom, and curing every disease and illness. … "For Jerusalem I will pick out a bearer of the glad tidings." *Is 41:26, Jn 8:58, Mt 9:35, Is 41:27*

Our Father…

"Who gives one man speech and makes another deaf and dumb? Or who gives sight to one and makes another blind? Is it not I, the LORD?" *Ex 4:11*

Hail Mary…

"Fear not, Abram! / I am your shield." … "I am the LORD who brought you from Ur … to give you this land as a possession." *Gn 15:1,7*

Hail Mary…

"Know that I am with you; I will protect you wherever you go." … [Y]ou shall be holy, because I am holy. *Gn 28:15, Lv 11:45*

Hail Mary…

"I will receive glory through Pharaoh and all his army, and the Egyptians will know I am the LORD." *Ex 14:4*

Hail Mary…

He brought us out of Egypt with his strong hand and outstretched arm, with terrifying power, with signs and wonders; and bringing us into this country, he gave us this land flowing with milk and honey. *Dt 26:8-9*

Hail Mary…

The LORD will remove all sickness from you; he will not afflict you with any of the malignant diseases that you know from Egypt. *Dt 7:15*

Hail Mary…

"May the LORD, the God of the spirits of all mankind, set over the community a man who shall act as their leader in all things, to guide them in all their actions; that the LORD's community may not be like sheep without a shepherd." *Nm 27:16-17*

Hail Mary…

The LORD, your God, you shall worship; … I will remove all sickness from your midst. *Ex 23:25*

Hail Mary…

"This is the law for the victim of leprosy at the time of his purification. He shall be brought to the priest, who is to go outside the camp to examine him." … "In an attack of leprosy you shall be careful to observe exactly and to carry out all the directions of the levitical priests." *Lv 14:2-3, Dt 24:8*

Hail Mary…

"How long will this people spurn me? How long will they refuse to believe in me, despite all the signs I have performed among them?" *Nm 14:11*

Hail Mary… Glory Be… O My Jesus…

FIRE AND LIGHT

Moses heard the Word of God in the burning bush. Elijah reached heaven in the fiery chariot. Moses and Elijah joined Jesus at the top of the mountain. The glory of God shone forth white as light to the apostles, Peter, James, and John.

THE FOURTH LUMINOUS MYSTERY
THE TRANSFIGURATION

I am God, there is none like me. / At the beginning I foretell the outcome; / ... I accomplish my every purpose. ... Jesus took Peter, James, and John his brother, and led them up a high mountain by themselves. And he was transfigured before them. ... Moses and Elijah appeared to them, conversing with him. *Is 46:9-10, Mt 17:1-3*

Our Father...

Moses was tending the flock .... he came to Horeb, the mountain of God. There an angel of the LORD appeared to him in fire flaming out of a bush. *Ex 3:1-2*

Hail Mary...

God called out to him from the bush, "Moses! Moses!" ... Should there be a prophet among you, / ... in dreams will I speak to him; / Not so with my servant Moses! / Throughout my house he bears my trust: / face to face I speak to him. *Ex 3:4, Nm 12:6-8*

Hail Mary...

"I will be with you; and this shall be your proof that it is I who have sent you: when you bring my people out of Egypt, you will worship God on this very mountain." *Ex 3:12*

Hail Mary...

God replied, "I am who am." ... "This is what you shall tell the Israelites: I AM sent me to you." *Ex 3:14*

Hail Mary...

[Aaron and Moses] met at the mountain of God. ... Moses and Aaron went and assembled all the elders of the Israelites. ... The people believed, and when they heard that the LORD was concerned about them and had seen their affliction, they bowed down in worship. *Ex 4:27,29,31*

Hail Mary...

To the Israelites the glory of the LORD was seen as a consuming fire on the mountaintop. But Moses passed into the midst of the cloud. *Ex 24:17-18*

Hail Mary...

"For what mortal has heard, as we have, the voice of the living God speaking from the midst of fire, and survived?" ... [N]o prophet has arisen in Israel like Moses, whom the LORD knew face to face. He had no equal in all the signs and wonders the LORD sent him to perform. *Dt 5:26, Dt 34:10-11*

Hail Mary...

Moses stayed there with the LORD for forty days and forty nights. ... When the LORD had finished speaking to Moses on Mount Sinai, he gave him the two tablets of the commandments, the stone tablets inscribed by God's own finger. *Ex 34:28, Ex 31:18*

Hail Mary...

Moses came down from the mountain. ... He warned them, "Be ready for the third day." *Ex 19:14-15*

Hail Mary...

The LORD said to Moses, "Cut two stone tablets like the former, that I may write on them the commandments which were on the former tablets that you broke." *Ex 34:1*

Hail Mary... Glory Be... O My Jesus...

OUR DAILY BREAD

Every day the Israelites ate manna that rained down from heaven. Jesus, the Bread of Life, established the Eucharist as a memorial of his Passion and Death. We pray during Mass – "give us this day our daily bread."

THE FIFTH LUMINOUS MYSTERY
THE INSTITUTION OF THE EUCHARIST

Melchizedek, king of Salem and priest of God Most High, … without beginning of days or end of life, thus made to resemble the Son of God, he remains a priest forever. … This day shall be a memorial feast for you, which all your generations shall celebrate with pilgrimage to the LORD, as a perpetual institution. … On the first day of the Feast of Unleavened Bread, … Jesus took bread, said the blessing, … "Take and eat, this is my body." *Heb 7:1,3, Ex 12:14, Mt 26:17,26*

Our Father…

Noah built an altar to the LORD, and choosing from every clean animal…, he offered holocausts on the altar. *Gn 8:20*

Hail Mary…

Melchizedek, king of Salem, brought out bread and wine, and being a priest of God Most High, he blessed Abram with these words: / "Blessed be Abram by God Most High, / the creator of heaven and earth." *Gn 14:18-19*

Hail Mary…

Keep, then, this custom of the unleavened bread. … fine flour mixed with oil. … "This is the bread which the LORD has given you to eat." *Ex 12:17, Lv 2:5, Ex 16:15*

Hail Mary…

The LORD said to Moses, … "This month shall stand at the head of your calendar; … the first month of the year." *Ex 12:1-2*

Hail Mary…

Tell the whole community of Israel: On the tenth of the month every one of your families must procure for itself a lamb. *Ex 12:3*

Hail Mary…

The lamb must be a year-old male and without blemish. … [I]t shall be slaughtered during the evening twilight. … This is how you are to eat it: with your loins girt, sandals on your feet and your staff in hand. … It is the Passover of the LORD. *Ex 12:5-6, Ex 12:11*

Hail Mary…

"'This is the Passover sacrifice of the LORD, who passed over the houses of the Israelites of Egypt; when he struck down the Egyptians, he spared our houses.'" *Ex 12:27*

Hail Mary…

You shall offer the Passover sacrifice from your flock. … For seven days you shall eat with it only unleavened bread, the bread of affliction. *Dt 16:2-3*

Hail Mary…

He therefore let you be afflicted with hunger, and then fed you with manna, a food unknown to you and your fathers, in order to show you that not by bread alone does man live, but by every word that comes forth from the mouth of the LORD. *Dt 8:3*

Hail Mary…

[Y]ou nourished your people with food of angels / and furnished them bread from heaven. … The fire is to be kept burning continuously on the altar; it must not go out. *Wis 16:20, Lv 6:6*

Hail Mary… Glory Be… O My Jesus… Hail Holy Queen…

His Burden

Jesus triumphantly entered Jerusalem on a beast of burden. One week later He carried the burden of our sins to Calvary. Ironically, many people in both of these crowds were the same — one week cheering, the next week jeering.

THE SORROWFUL MYSTERIES

The Sign of the Cross
The Apostles' Creed

[T]he LORD said, "I have witnessed the affliction of my people in Egypt and have heard their cry of complaint against their slave drivers, so I know well what they are suffering. Therefore I have come down to rescue them." ... [Y]ou also testify, because you have been with me from the beginning. *Ex 3:7-8, Jn 15:27*

Our Father...

[B]ecause of his fidelity to the oath he had sworn to your fathers, ... he brought you out with his strong hand from the place of slavery. *Dt 7:8*

Hail Mary...

Trust God and he will help you; / make straight your ways and hope in him. ... Woe to you who have lost hope! *Sir 2:6,14*

Hail Mary...

Choose life, then, that you and your descendants may live, by loving the LORD, your God, heeding his voice, and holding fast to him. *Dt 30:19*

Hail Mary... Glory Be...

MY ROCK, MY SALVATION

While Jesus prayed in the Garden of Gethsemane, the apostles slept. Jesus, drenched in blood, leaned in agony on the rock and received strength from an angel as He accepted the cup — God's will to save His people. Three days later, two angels at Jesus' empty tomb greeted Mary Magdalene and she then rushed to tell the Good News to the apostles.

28

THE FIRST SORROWFUL MYSTERY
THE AGONY IN THE GARDEN

In the beginning, … the LORD God planted a garden in Eden, in the east, and he placed there the man [Adam] whom he had formed. … Jesus went out … to where there was a garden. … He was in such agony … his sweat became like drops of blood falling on the ground. … Judas his betrayer also knew the place, because Jesus had often met there with his disciples. … *Gn 1:1, Gn 2:8, Jn 18:1, Lk 22:44, Jn 18:2*

Our Father…

This was a night of vigil for the LORD, … so on this same night all the Israelites must keep a vigil for the LORD throughout their generations. *Ex 12:42*

Hail Mary…

"Throughout your generations this atonement is to be made once a year with the blood of the atoning sin offering. This altar is most sacred to the LORD." *Ex 30:10*

Hail Mary…

Fear not death's decree for you; / remember, it embraces those before you, and those after. / Thus God has ordained for all flesh; / why then should you reject the will of the Most High? *Sir 41:3-4*

Hail Mary…

[He] stretched forth his hand for the cup, / to offer blood of the grape, / And poured it out at the foot of the altar, / a sweet-smelling odor to the Most High God. *Sir 50:15*

Hail Mary…

I will ever praise your name / and be constant in my prayers to you. *Sir 51:11*

Hail Mary…

LORD, Father and God of my life, / abandon me not into their control! … Therefore I prayed, and prudence was given me; / I pleaded, and the spirit of Wisdom came to me. *Sir 23:4, Wis 7:7*

Hail Mary…

[I]t is the blood, as the seat of life, that makes atonement. *Lv 17:11*

Hail Mary…

"This is the blood of the covenant which the LORD has made with you." *Ex 24:8*

Hail Mary…

The rest of the blood he shall pour out at the base of the altar of holocausts which is at the entrance of the meeting tent. … Thus the priest shall make atonement for them, and they will be forgiven. *Lv 4:18,20*

Hail Mary…

The evidence of a single witness is not sufficient for putting a person to death. *Nm 35:30*

Hail Mary… Glory Be… O My Jesus…

XL

Both Jesus and St. Paul suffered brutal scourging and abuses at the hands of the Romans. If we live St. Paul's exhortation to "imitate Christ", we can expect persecutions in this world yet hope in the promise of eternal life in the New Jerusalem.

THE SECOND SORROWFUL MYSTERY
THE SCOURGING AT THE PILLAR

Jesus knew from the beginning the ones who would not believe and the one who would betray him. … It was the wicked who with hands and words invited death. … One witness alone shall not take the stand against a man; … a judicial fact shall be established only on the testimony of two or three witnesses. … [Judas said,] "I have sinned in betraying innocent blood." *Jn 6:64, Wis 1:16, Dt 19:15, Mt 27:4*

Our Father…

[T]hirty shekels of silver. … Accept whatever befalls you, / in crushing misfortune be patient. *Ex 21:32, Sir 2:4*

Hail Mary…

A patient man need stand firm but for a time, / and then contentment comes back to him. *Sir 1:20*

Hail Mary…

No evil can harm the man who fears the LORD; / through trials, again and again he is safe. *Sir 33:1*

Hail Mary…

Forty stripes may be given him, but no more; lest, if he were beaten with more stripes than these, your kinsman should be looked upon as disgraced because of the severity of the beating. *Dt 25:3*

Hail Mary…

[F]rom man in regard to his fellow man I will demand an accounting for human life. *Gn 9:5*

Hail Mary…

The LORD has commanded that what has been done today be done to make atonement for you. *Lv 8:34*

Hail Mary…

Close at hand is the day of their disaster, / and their doom is rushing upon them! *Dt 32:35*

Hail Mary…

In your distress, when all these things shall have come upon you, you shall finally return to the LORD, your God, and heed his voice. *Dt 4:30*

Hail Mary…

For if before men, indeed, they be punished, / yet is their hope full of immortality; / … God tried them / and found them worthy of himself. *Wis 3:4-5*

Hail Mary…

"You shall not repeat a false report. Do not join the wicked in putting your hand, as an unjust witness, upon anyone." *Ex 23:1*

Hail Mary… Glory Be… O My Jesus…

CLEANSING TEARS

Mary Magdalene's tears of repentance and sorrow washed Jesus' feet from the dirt and grime of the streets. The passion and sufferings of Jesus Christ wash away our sins through the gift of His forgiveness and Divine Mercy.

THE THIRD SORROWFUL MYSTERY
THE CROWNING WITH THORNS

In the beginning, ... God created man in his image; / in the divine image he created him. ... If anyone sheds the blood of man, / by man shall his blood be shed; / For in the image of God / has man been made. ... Pilate addressed them a third time, "What evil has this man done? I found him guilty of no capital crime." ... According to the law almost everything is purified by blood, and without the shedding of blood there is no forgiveness. *Gn 1:1,27, Gn 9:6, Lk 23:22, Heb 9:22*

Our Father...

The testimony of two or three witnesses is required for putting a person to death. ... At the execution, the witnesses are to be the first to raise their hands against him. *Dt 17:6-7*

Hail Mary...

"You shall not kill." ... "You shall not bear false witness against your neighbor." *Ex 20:13,16*

Hail Mary...

In rendering judgment, do not consider who a person is; give ear to the lowly and to the great alike, fearing no man, for judgment is God's. *Dt 1:17*

Hail Mary...

[W]hen you come to serve the LORD, / prepare yourself for trials. / Be sincere of heart and steadfast, / undisturbed in time of adversity. *Sir 2:1-2*

Hail Mary...

"How long will this wicked community grumble against me? I have heard the grumblings of the Israelites against me." *Nm 14:27*

Hail Mary...

With revilement and torture let us put him to the test / that we may have proof of his gentleness / and try his patience. *Wis 2:19*

Hail Mary...

Seek not from the LORD authority, / nor from the king a place of honor. / Parade not your justice before the LORD, / and before the king flaunt not your wisdom. ... Be swift to hear, / but slow to answer. *Sir 7:4-5, Sir 5:13*

Hail Mary...

[T]hey stripped him of the long tunic he had on ... [and] dipped the tunic in its blood. ... [F]alse charges in public, trial before all the people, / and lying testimony are harder to bear than death. *Gn 37:23,31, Sir 26:5*

Hail Mary...

A faithful God, without deceit, / how just and upright he is! / Yet basely has he been treated by his degenerate children, / a perverse and crooked race! *Dt 32:4-5*

Hail Mary...

"I am who am." ... Even to the death fight for truth, / and the LORD your God will battle for you. *Ex 3:14, Sir 4:28*

Hail Mary... Glory Be... O My Jesus...

HIS BURDEN

Jesus triumphantly entered Jerusalem on a beast of burden. One week later He carried the burden of our sins to Calvary. Ironically, many people in both of these crowds were the same — one week cheering, the next week jeering.

THE FOURTH SORROWFUL MYSTERY
THE CARRYING OF THE CROSS

In the beginning, ... God said, "Let the earth bring forth vegetation: ... every kind of fruit tree on earth." ... God made various trees ... with the tree of life in the middle of the garden and the tree of the knowledge of good and bad. ... For blest is the wood through which justice comes about. ... [C]arrying the cross himself he went out to ... Golgotha. *Gn 1:1,11, Gn 2:9, Wis 14:7, Jn 19:17*

Our Father...

Abraham took the wood for the holocaust and laid it on his son Isaac's shoulders. ... "Here are the fire and the wood, but where is the sheep for the holocaust?" "Son," Abraham answered, "God himself will provide the sheep for the holocaust." *Gn 22:6-8*

Hail Mary...

When the Egyptians maltreated and oppressed us, imposing hard labor upon us, we cried to the LORD, the God of our fathers, and he heard our cry and saw our affliction, our toil and our oppression. *Dt 26:6-7*

Hail Mary...

Moses again had recourse to the LORD and said, "Lord, why do you treat this people so badly? And why did you send me on such a mission?" *Ex 5:22*

Hail Mary...

[Y]our burden will be lightened, since they will bear it with you. ... Most important of all, pray to God / to set your feet in the path of truth. *Ex 18:22, Sir 37:15*

Hail Mary...

The LORD, your God, shall you follow, and him shall you fear; his commandment shall you observe, and his voice shall you heed, serving him and holding fast to him alone. *Dt 13:5*

Hail Mary...

Work at your tasks in due season, / and in his own time God will give you your reward. ... "Be brave and steadfast; have no fear or dread of them, for it is the LORD, your God, who marches with you; he will never fail you or forsake you." *Sir 51:30, Dt 31:6*

Hail Mary...

Do not the tears that stream down her cheek / cry out against him that causes them to fall? / He who serves God willingly is heard; / his petition reaches the heavens. *Sir 35:15-16*

Hail Mary...

Trust God and he will help you; / make straight your ways and hope in him. ... He who does a kindness is remembered afterward; / when he falls, he finds a support. *Sir 2:6, Sir 3:30*

Hail Mary...

He bent his shoulder to the burden. ... Let us condemn him to a shameful death; / for according to his own words, God will take care of him. *Gn 49:15, Wis 2:20*

Hail Mary...

[T]he souls of the just are in the hand of God, / ... and their passing away was thought an affliction. / ... But they are in peace. *Wis 3:1-3*

Hail Mary... Glory Be... O My Jesus...

First Born, Pierced with a Sword

In faithful obedience Abraham prepared to sacrifice his first-born son Isaac. Mary and Joseph's obedience to the Mosaic law prefigured the ultimate sacrifice of Christ as "the Lamb of God."

The Fifth Sorrowful Mystery
The Crucifixion

What was from the beginning, / ... what we have seen with our eyes, / ... our fellowship is with the Father / and with his Son, Jesus Christ. ... Solomon began to build the house of the LORD in Jerusalem on Mount Moriah. ... The ark of the commandments you shall bring inside, behind this veil which divides the holy place from the holy of holies. ... Then the veil of the temple was torn down the middle. Jesus cried out in a loud voice, "Father, into your hands I commend my spirit." *1 Jn 1:1,3, 2 Chr 3:1, Ex 26:33, Lk 23:45-46*

Our Father...

Abel, for his part, brought one of the best firstlings of his flock. The LORD looked with favor on Abel and his offering. ... The lamb must be a year-old male and without blemish ... it shall be slaughtered during the evening twilight. *Gn 4:4, Ex 12:5-6*

Hail Mary...

God said: "Take your son ... offer him up as a holocaust on a height that I will point out to you." *Gn 22:2*

Hail Mary...

"Thus shall Aaron offer up the bullock, his sin offering, to atone for himself and for his family. When he has slaughtered it, he shall take a censer full of glowing embers from the altar before the LORD." *Lv 16:11-12*

Hail Mary...

"These are the regulations for the Passover. ... You shall not break any of its bones. The whole community of Israel must keep this feast." *Ex 12:43,46-47*

Hail Mary...

"God himself will provide the [lamb] for the holocaust." ... As an oblation you shall offer a holocaust to the LORD, ... yearling lambs that you are sure are unblemished. *Gn 22:8, Nm 28:19*

Hail Mary...

Will you not leave your riches to others, / and your earnings to be divided by lot? *Sir 14:15*

Hail Mary...

And you gave your sons good ground for hope / that you would permit repentance for their sins. ... How great the mercy of the LORD, / his forgiveness of those who return to him! *Wis 12:19, Sir 17:24*

Hail Mary...

Next he tied up his son Isaac, and put him on top of the wood on the altar. Then he reached out and took the knife to slaughter his son. ... "... Abraham!" ... "Do not do the least thing to him. I know now how devoted you are to God, since you did not withhold from me your own beloved son." *Gn 22:9-12*

Hail Mary...

[Moses] took the blood and sprinkled it on the people, saying, "This is the blood of the covenant which the LORD has made with you." ... When the people witnessed the thunder and lightning, the trumpet blast and the mountain smoking, they all feared and trembled. ... I am the LORD. ... I will rescue you by my outstretched arm. *Ex 24:8, Ex 20:18, Ex 6:6*

Hail Mary...

[His corpse] shall not remain on the tree overnight. You shall bury it the same day; otherwise, since God's curse rests on him who hangs on a tree, you will defile the land which the LORD, your God, is giving you as an inheritance. *Dt 21:23*

> *Hail Mary... Glory Be... O My Jesus...*
> *Hail Holy Queen...*

WOMAN

Entangled in the serpent's lie, Eve at the foot of a tree brought death to the world as she shared in the first sin with Adam. At the foot of the cross, the New Eve, the Blessed Virgin Mary, crushed the head of the serpent, while the New Adam conquered death.

MY ROCK, MY SALVATION

While Jesus prayed in the Garden of Gethsemane, the apostles slept. Jesus, drenched in blood, leaned in agony on the rock and received strength from an angel as He accepted the cup — God's will to save His people. Three days later, two angels at Jesus' empty tomb greeted Mary Magdalene and she then rushed to tell the Good News to the apostles.

THE GLORIOUS MYSTERIES

The Sign of the Cross

The Apostles' Creed

The clear vault of the sky shines forth / like heaven itself, a vision of glory. ... Who has performed these deeds? / He who has called forth the generations since the beginning. / I, the LORD, am the first. ... Sing to the LORD, for he is gloriously triumphant. *Sir 43:1, Is 41:4, Ex 15:21*

Our Father...

Understand, then, that the LORD, your God, is God indeed, the faithful God who keeps his merciful covenant down to the thousandth generation. *Dt 7:9*

Hail Mary...

You who fear the LORD, hope for good things, / for lasting joy and mercy. *Sir 2:9*

Hail Mary...

Those who serve her serve the Holy One; / those who love her the LORD loves. *Sir 4:14*

Hail Mary... Glory Be...

THREE DAYS

Numerous times Christ referred to Himself fulfilling prophesies. While Jonah spent three days in the belly of a whale so Jesus said He would spend three days in the depths of Hell.

THE FIRST GLORIOUS MYSTERY
THE RESURRECTION

He is the beginning, the firstborn from the dead, / that in all things he himself might be preeminent. ... [B]e ready for the third day; for on the third day the LORD will come down on Mount Sinai before the eyes of all the people .... On the morning of the third day there were peals of thunder and lightning, and a heavy cloud over the mountain, and a very loud trumpet blast. ... Then beginning with Moses and all the prophets, he interpreted to them what referred to him in all the scriptures. *Col 1:18, Ex 19:11,16, Lk 24:27*

Our Father...

All the fountains of the great abyss burst forth, / and the floodgates of the sky were opened. *Gn 7:11*

Hail Mary...

She went down with him into the dungeon, / and did not desert him in his bonds, / Until she brought him the scepter of royalty / and authority over his oppressors. *Wis 10:14*

Hail Mary...

[T]he days of eternity: who can number these? / Heaven's height, earth's breadth, / the depths of the abyss: who can explore these? *Sir 1:2-3*

Hail Mary...

For love of your fathers he chose their descendants and personally led you out of Egypt by his great power. *Dt 4:37*

Hail Mary...

Limited are the days of one man's life, / but the life of Israel is days without number. *Sir 37:23*

Hail Mary...

If you do good, know for whom you are doing it, / and your kindness will have its effect. *Sir 12:1*

Hail Mary...

In life he performed wonders, / and after death, marvelous deeds. *Sir 48:14*

Hail Mary...

Among brethren their leader is in honor; / he who fears God is in honor among his people. *Sir 10:20*

Hail Mary...

For I will sing the LORD's renown. / Oh, proclaim the greatness of our God! *Dt 32:3*

Hail Mary...

"I, the LORD, am your God." ... In the highest heavens did I dwell, / my throne on a pillar of cloud. / The vault of heaven I compassed alone, / through the deep abyss I wandered. *Ex 20:2, Sir 24:4-5*

Hail Mary... Glory Be... O My Jesus...

THE RIGHT HAND OF GOD

With the Egyptians in pursuit, Moses and the Israelites crossed the Red Sea and trusted in God's promise to save them and bring them to the Promised Land. The crucified Christ poured forth water and blood to wash us clean. Through His Divine Mercy, He brought salvation and hope in eternal life.

THE SECOND GLORIOUS MYSTERY
THE ASCENSION

Was it not foretold you from the beginning? / … Since the earth was founded / He sits enthroned above the vault of the earth. … He was in the beginning with God. / All things came to be through him, / and without him nothing came to be. … … "I say to you, you will see the sky opened and the angels of God ascending and descending on the Son of Man." *Is 40:21-22, Jn 1:2-3, Jn 1:51*

Our Father...

"I, the LORD, am your God, who brought you out of the land of Egypt. … You shall not have other gods besides me." *Ex 20:2-3*

Hail Mary...

The heavens, even the highest heavens, belong to the LORD, your God, as well as the earth and everything on it. *Dt 10:14*

Hail Mary...

All wisdom comes from the LORD. / … There is but one, wise and truly awe-inspiring, / seated upon his throne. *Sir 1:1,6*

Hail Mary...

The LORD shall reign forever and ever. *Ex 15:18*

Hail Mary...

All that is of earth returns to earth, / and what is from above returns above. *Sir 40:11*

Hail Mary...

Whenever the ark set out, Moses would say, / "Arise, O LORD, that your enemies may be scattered, / and those who hate you may flee before you." *Nm 10:35*

Hail Mary...

And when it came to rest, he would say, / "Return, O LORD, you who ride upon the clouds, / to the troops of Israel." *Nm 10:36*

Hail Mary...

Who is like to you among the gods, O LORD? / Who is like to you, magnificent in holiness? *Ex 15:11*

Hail Mary...

The LORD will open up for you his rich treasure house of the heavens. *Dt 28:12*

Hail Mary...

This is why you must now know, and fix in your heart, that the LORD is God in the heavens above and the earth below, and that there is no other. *Dt 4:39*

Hail Mary… Glory Be… O My Jesus...

SPIRIT IN THE CHURCH

The Holy Spirit's love filled the Apostles and the other followers of Jesus, and they proceeded to the ends of the earth to preach the Word of God. The Spirit's flame continued throughout the centuries as evidenced by the lives of saints, such as, St. Thomas Aquinas, St. Augustine, St. Francis of Assisi, and St. Teresa of Avila.

THE THIRD GLORIOUS MYSTERY
THE DESCENT OF THE HOLY SPIRIT

In the beginning, … a mighty wind swept over the waters. … Beginning with the day after the sabbath … and then on the day after the seventh week, the fiftieth day, you shall present the new cereal offering to the LORD. … Thus did Moses announce to the Israelites the festivals of the LORD. … [T]he holy Spirit fell upon them as it had upon us at the beginning. *Gn 1:1-2, Lv 23:15-16,44, Acts 11:15*

Our Father...

To the Israelites the glory of the LORD was seen as a consuming fire on the mountaintop. … It was always so: during the day the Dwelling was covered by the cloud, which at night had the appearance of fire. *Ex 24:17, Nm 9:16*

Hail Mary...

Out of the heavens he let you hear his voice to discipline you; on earth he let you see his great fire, and you heard him speaking out of the fire. *Dt 4:36*

Hail Mary...

[F]ix in your heart, that the LORD is God in the heavens above and on earth below, and that there is no other. *Dt 4:39*

Hail Mary...

The LORD, our God, has indeed let us see his glory and his majesty! We have heard his voice from the midst of the fire. … Taking some of the spirit that was on Moses, he bestowed it on the seventy elders; and as the spirit came to rest on them, they prophesied. *Dt 5:24, Nm 11:25*

Hail Mary...

For the LORD, your God, is a consuming fire, a jealous God. *Dt 4:24*

Hail Mary...

Ever present in your midst, I will be your God, and you will be my people; for it is I, the LORD, your God, who brought you out of the land of the Egyptians. *Lv 26:12-13*

Hail Mary...

For the spirit of the LORD fills the world, / is all-embracing, and knows what man says. *Wis 1:7*

Hail Mary...

Let your spirits rejoice in the mercy of God, / and be not ashamed to give him praise. *Sir 51:29*

Hail Mary...

Woe to you who have lost hope! / what will you do at the visitation of the LORD? *Sir 2:14*

Hail Mary...

[Y]ou furnished the flaming pillar / which was a guide on the unknown way. *Wis 18:3*

Hail Mary... Glory Be... O My Jesus...

MAGNIFICAT

The Sorrowful Mother's journey led her to the foot of the cross. However, her eyes were ever on heaven where her Risen Son welcomed her. The Resurrected Christ beckons each one of us to eternal life.

The Fourth Glorious Mystery
The Assumption of the
Blessed Virgin Mary into Heaven

[H]e chose us in him, before the foundation of the world, to be holy and without blemish before him. ...[Jacob] had a dream: a stairway rested on the ground, with its top reaching to the heavens; and God's messengers were going up and down on it. ... Mary said: / ... "The Mighty One has done great things for me." *Eph 1:4, Gn 28:12, Lk 1:46,49*

Our Father...

Enoch walked with God, and he was no longer here, for God took him. ... Few on earth have been made the equal of ENOCH, for he was taken up bodily. *Gn 5:24, Sir 49 :14*

Hail Mary...

Moses then went up with Aaron ... and they beheld the God of Israel. Under his feet there appeared to be sapphire tilework, as clear as the sky itself. *Ex 24: 9-10*

Hail Mary...

In your mercy you led the people you redeemed; / in your strength you guided them to your holy dwelling. *Ex 15:13*

Hail Mary...

The LORD bless you and keep you! / The LORD let his face shine upon you, and be gracious to you! *Nm 6:24-25*

Hail Mary...

The prayer of the lowly pierces the clouds; / it does not rest till it reaches its goal. *Sir 35:17*

Hail Mary...

For great is the power of God; / by the humble he is glorified. ... For those who keep the holy precepts hallowed shall be found holy. *Sir 3:19, Wis 6:10*

Hail Mary...

To observe her laws is the basis for incorruptibility; / and incorruptibility makes one close to God. *Wis 6:18-19*

Hail Mary...

For she is an aura of the might of God / and a pure effusion of the glory of the Almighty; / therefore nought that is sullied enters into her. *Wis 7:25*

Hail Mary...

For she is the refulgence of eternal light, / the spotless mirror of the power of God, / the image of his goodness. *Wis 7:26*

Hail Mary...

For she is fairer than the sun / and surpasses every constellation of the stars. ... In whatever you do, remember your last days, / and you will never sin. *Wis 7:29, Sir 7:36*

Hail Mary... Glory Be... O My Jesus...

SHEPHERD AND KING

Bethlehem, home of King David and his son King Solomon, was the birthplace of the King of Kings. As Mary and Joseph, both of the Davidic lineage, held the Prince of Peace, the three kings, as well as, lowly shepherds adored Jesus. The Good Shepherd's care extends to all of His flock - rich and poor alike.

THE FIFTH GLORIOUS MYSTERY
THE CORONATION OF MARY, QUEEN OF HEAVEN AND EARTH

In the beginning, ... God made the two great lights, the greater one to govern the day, and the lesser one to govern the night; and he made the stars. ... A great sign appeared in the sky, a woman clothed with the sun, with the moon under her feet, and on her head a crown of twelve stars. ... Night will be no more, nor will they need light from lamp or sun, for the Lord God shall give them light, and they shall reign forever and ever. *Gn 1:1,16, Rv 12:1, Rv 22:5*

Our Father...

"Honor ... your mother." ... The God of your father, who helps you, / God Almighty, who blesses you, / With the blessings of the heavens above. *Ex 20:12, Gn 49:25*

Hail Mary...

"[H]e will then raise you high in praise and renown and glory above all other nations he has made, and you will be a people sacred to the LORD, your God, as he promised." *Dt 26:19*

Hail Mary...

Fear of the LORD is glory and splendor, / gladness and a festive crown. *Sir 1:9*

Hail Mary...

There is but one, wise and truly awe-inspiring, / seated upon his throne: / It is the LORD; he created her, / has seen her and taken note of her. *Sir 1:6-7*

Hail Mary...

For great is the power of God; / by the humble he is glorified. ... [B]less the LORD / who has crowned you with glory! *Sir 3:19, Sir 45:26*

Hail Mary...

"You, Judah, shall your brothers praise. ... The scepter shall never depart from Judah." ... [T]hey receive the splendid crown, / the beauteous diadem, from the hand of the LORD. *Gn 49:8,10, Wis 5:16*

Hail Mary...

Resplendent and unfading is Wisdom, / and she is readily perceived by those who love her, / and found by those who seek her. *Wis 6:12*

Hail Mary...

I give you thanks, O God of my father; / I praise you, O God my savior! ... [T]he faithful shall abide with him in love: / Because grace and mercy are with his holy ones. *Sir 51:1, Wis 3:9*

Hail Mary...

Those who serve her serve the Holy One; / those who love her the LORD loves. *Sir 4:14*

Hail Mary...

The heavens, even the highest heavens, belong to the LORD, your God, as well as the earth and everything on it. *Dt 10:14*

Hail Mary... Glory Be... O My Jesus...
Hail Holy Queen...

AUTHOR'S NOTE

Fifty years ago, the crew of Apollo 8 read from the Book of Genesis as they orbited the moon. Astronauts Bill Anders, Jim Lovell, and Frank Borman recited Genesis chapter 1, verses 1 through 10. They started with "In the beginning, God created..." and they concluded with "God bless all of you, all of you on the good Earth." As I reflect over these last fifty years, how far we have strayed from the sense of God as Creator, God as the Almighty. The loss of the sacred, especially at Christmastime, can be disheartening and a little sad. However, we can look to all of creation and the mystery of our redemption with profound joy. Like those astronauts some fifty years ago, who recited the words "In the beginning...," we too know that the God who has no beginning, gave us the breath of life and formed our world out of nothing.

We do not have to travel to the moon to see the God of Creation. But to know God we must spend time with him. Spend time in prayer with him. A most profound prayer to understand the God who created us and also redeemed us is the Most Holy Rosary. I have been writing scriptural prayers books for nearly 30 years, and yet each day immersed in Scripture unveils yet another aspect of the profound wonder of God as seen through the lens of the Rosary – the significant events of the life of Mary and Jesus.

In the 1990s, I wrote From Genesis to Revelation. This prayer book was a collection of seven scriptural rosaries based on selections from the entirety of Sacred Scriptures. This rosary meditation prayer book was based on thematic collections, such as, the 150 Psalms, the Prophets, the Blessed Words of Jesus and Mary, and the writings of St. Paul.

A Scriptural Rosary simplifies, yet spiritually edifies, the meditation process of the praying of the Most Holy Rosary. A Scriptural Rosary is a conversation with God. He speaks to us through His Word and we respond with the Our Father, or the Angelic salutation, the Hail Mary. Sacred Scriptures are added to the praying of the Most Holy Rosary to keep us alert, to help us understand the mysteries, and to converse with God in the presence of His Blessed Mother.

For many centuries, the Most Holy Rosary consisted of fifteen decades prayed in three groups of mysteries - the Joyful, the Sorrowful, and the Glorious. Pope Saint John Paul II in his 2002 Apostolic Letter *Rosarium Virginis Mariae* recommended praying a new set of mysteries called the Luminous Mysteries. The Luminous Mysteries filled in the chronological gap from the Fifth Joyful Mystery with Jesus as a boy of twelve to the First Sorrowful Mystery when Jesus begins His Passion in the Garden of Gethsemane. The Luminous Mysteries complement the Joyful, Sorrowful, and Glorious Mysteries.

For some, the addition of the Luminous Mysteries may cause concern because of the departure from tradition. Rather we should be renewed and energized by the addition of these new Luminous Mysteries, looking forward to a revitalization of the praying of the Most Holy Rosary. Over the years, I have had many requests to update the Seven Scriptural Rosaries in From Genesis to Revelation with meditations for the Luminous Mysteries.

First, in 2004, <u>The Psalter of Jesus and Mary</u> updated Book 4: The Psalms in <u>From Genesis to Revelation</u>. The Joyful, Sorrowful, and Glorious scriptural mysteries remained the same 150 Psalms, as presented in Book Four. To unveil the new Luminous Mysteries in light of Scripture, I selected meditations from the thirty-one Proverbs, the wise words of Solomon.

Next, in 2009, <u>Pearls of Peace</u> updated Book 6: SS Peter and Paul in <u>From Genesis to Revelation</u>. Pope Emeritus Benedict XVI declared a Jubilee Year of St. Paul from June 2008 through June 2009. It was during that jubilee year that the selections for the Luminous Mysteries were completed. The Our Father scripture meditations focused on praying for peace. Additionally, each Our Father meditation recalled the holy places where Jesus lived, preached, taught, and died. The Hail Mary verses remained the same selections from the epistles of St. Paul. New St. Paul reflections were selected for the Luminous Mysteries. Keeping with the theme of Jesus' life on earth, this prayer book was illustrated with photography from the Holy Land.

Now, in 2019, I focus on the theme of Creation and how "In the beginning..." is a unifying theme to meditate on the entirety of the Gospels as reflected in the mysteries of the Most Holy Rosary. This book, "In the Beginning…", updates Book 1: The Pentateuch in <u>From Genesis to Revelation</u>. The Our Father meditations are selected from Sacred Scripture verses that focus on "In the Beginning…". The Hail Mary meditations are selected from the Pentateuch [Genesis, Exodus, Leviticus, Numbers, and Deuteronomy]. Additional verses are selected from the Catholic Old Testament books of Wisdom and Sirach. All new meditations for the Luminous Mysteries were selected for this book.

In closing, I would like to extend a special thank you to Father Michael Duesterhaus, Diocese of Arlington, for his wise counsel. Without his efforts to keep me focused and thinking about the "things above," these prayer books would never have been possible.

Christine Haapala

Fairfax, Virginia

HOW TO PRAY THE MOST HOLY ROSARY

While holding the Crucifix in the hand, make the Sign of the Cross and recite the Apostles' Creed. On the first large bead, recite the Our Father. On the three small beads recite the Hail Mary for an increase in the three theological virtues of faith, hope, and love, next pray the Glory Be. On the larger bead mention and reflect on the mystery and recite the Our Father. On the decade of ten small beads meditate on the mystery and recite on each bead the Hail Mary. In closing each decade, recite the Glory Be followed by the O My Jesus prayer. Repeat this sequence of prayers for five decades. Conclude the Most Holy Rosary by praying the Hail, Holy Queen.

For many centuries, the Most Holy Rosary was prayed in three sets of mysteries – the Joyful, Sorrowful, and the Glorious. Pope Saint John Paul II in his Apostolic Letter Rosarium Virginis Mariae recommended an additional set of mysteries, the Luminous Mysteries.

While a complete Rosary consists of praying all twenty mysteries, it is more typical of group prayer to only pray five decades at a time. For children or beginners, a five- or twenty-decade Rosary may be too daunting, so begin praying with just one decade. While praying include reading of Sacred Scriptures about each mystery to bring the melody of prayer alive with mental pictures of persons, places, and events.

Originally, the Joyful Mysteries were prayed on Monday and Thursday, the Sorrowful Mysteries on Tuesday and Friday, and the Glorious Mysteries on Wednesday, Saturday, and Sunday. With the addition of the Luminous Mysteries, Pope Saint John Paul II recommended the Joyful Mysteries be prayed on Saturday and the Luminous Mysteries on Thursday.

The Prayers of the Most Holy Rosary

The Apostles' Creed

I believe in God, the Father almighty, Creator of heaven and earth, and in Jesus Christ, his only Son, our Lord, who was conceived by the Holy Spirit, born of the Virgin Mary, suffered under Pontius Pilate, was crucified, died and was buried; he descended into hell; on the third day he rose again from the dead; he ascended into heaven, and is seated at the right hand of God the Father almighty; from there he will come to judge the living and the dead. I believe in the Holy Spirit, the holy catholic Church, the communion of saints, the forgiveness of sins, the resurrection of the body, and life everlasting. Amen.

Our Father

Our Father, Who art in Heaven, hallowed be Thy Name. Thy kingdom come; Thy will be done on earth as it is in Heaven. Give us this day our daily bread, and forgive us our trespasses, as we forgive those who trespass against us. And lead us not into temptation, but deliver us from evil. Amen.

Hail Mary

Hail Mary, full of grace, the Lord is with thee; blessed art thou among women, and blessed is the Fruit of thy womb, Jesus. Holy Mary, Mother of God, pray for us sinners, now and at the hour of our death. Amen.

Doxology (Glory be)

Glory be to the Father, and to the Son, and to the Holy Spirit. As it was in the beginning, is now, and ever shall be, world without end. Amen

The Fatima Prayer

O My Jesus, forgive us our sins; save us from the fires of Hell, lead all souls to Heaven, especially those who are in most need of Thy Mercy.

Hail, Holy Queen

Hail, holy Queen, Mother of mercy, our life, our sweetness and our hope. To thee do we cry, poor banished children of Eve! To thee do we send up our sighs, mourning and weeping in this valley of tears. Turn then, most gracious advocate, thine eyes of mercy towards us. And after this, our exile, show unto us the blessed Fruit of thy womb, Jesus. O clement, O loving, O sweet Virgin Mary.

V. Pray for us, O holy Mother of God

R. That we may be made worthy of the promises of Christ.

Prayer after the Rosary

O God, whose only begotten Son, by His life, death and resurrection, has purchased for us the rewards of eternal life; grant, we beseech Thee, that, meditating upon these mysteries of the Most Holy Rosary of the Blessed Virgin Mary, we may imitate what they contain and obtain what they promise, through the same Christ our Lord. Amen.

OTHER WORKS BY CHRISTINE HAAPALA

PRAYER BOOKS FOR CHILDREN

Speak, Lord, I am Listening *A Scriptural Rosary Book*

Follow Me *A Scriptural Stations of the Cross Book*

PRAYER BOOKS FOR TEENS AND ADULTS

The Psalter of Jesus and Mary *A Scriptural Rosary according to Psalms and Proverbs*

Pearls of Peace *A Rosary Journey through the Holy Land*

The Suffering Servant's Courage *A Scriptural Rosary Book*

From Genesis to Revelation *Seven Scriptural Rosaries*

Seraphim and Cherubim *A Scriptural Chaplet of the Holy Angels*

In His Presence *Seven Visits to the Blessed Sacrament*

Sanctify my Heart *A Scriptural Novena to the Holy Spirit*

His Sorrowful Passion *Scriptural Chaplets of Divine Mercy*

PRAYER CDS

The Sanctity of Life *Scriptural Rosary CD*

Time for Mercy *A Scriptural Chaplet of Divine Mercy*

ORDERING INFORMATION

To purchase additional copies of this book or the other works mentioned above, please visit your local Catholic bookstore or on-line at www.sufferingservant.com.